Crossword
Age 10 up
90 Crossword Easy Puzzle Books for Kids

Copyright: Published in the United States by Nancy Dyer / © 2018 Nancy Dyer
All right reserved.

All rights reserved. No part of this publication may be reproduced, stored in retrieval system, copied in any form or by any means, electronic, mechanical, photocopying, recording or otherwise transmitted without written permission from the publisher. Please do not participate in or encourage piracy of this material in any way. You must not circulate this book in any format. Nancy Dyer Kids does not control or direct users' actions and is not responsible for the information or content shared, harm and/or actions of the book readers.

In accordance with the U.S. Copyright Act of 1976, the scanning, uploading and electronic sharing of any part of this book without the permission of the publisher constitute unlawful piracy and theft of the author's intellectual property. If you would like to use material from the book (other than just simply for reviewing the book), prior permission must be obtained by contacting the author at funspaceclub18@gmail.com
Thank you for your support of the author's rights.

This book includes free bonus that are available here:
www.funspace.club
Follow us: facebook.com/funspaceclub

Introduction

This crosswords puzzle book contain English words for kids 10+ years olds. Crosswords is a very easy and simple game. It's fun & educate kids. You just have to have a good stock of words. Look at empty boxes. By default, the game takes you through the clues in order starting with clue 1. After you fill in a clue you are taken to the next one. You have to fill up those across (horizontal) empty boxes and down (vertical) empty boxes with the right words and phrases by using clue to get idea.

See more great books for kids at

www.funspace.club

Follow us : facebook.com/funspaceclub

Send email to get answer & solution here : funspaceclub18@gmail.com

Geography

Across

2. _____ is the height of an area, measured from sea level.

3. The _____ is a figure-8-shaped diagram that shows the declination of the sun (the angle that the sun is from the equator), for each day in the year.

6. An _____ is a group or chain of islands clustered together in a sea or ocean.

7. _____ are a pair of points that are on opposite sides of a planet (like the north pole and the south pole).

Down

1. _____ circle is the _____ is an imaginary circle at latitude 66° 30' n, around the north pole.

2. _____ circle is the _____ is an imaginary circle at latitude 66° 30' s, around the south pole.

4. A book containing maps and charts.

5. An _____ is a ring (or partial ring) of coral that forms an island in an ocean or sea.

Food

Across

2. _____ is a dairy food made from milk.

5. _____ is a grain. Flour is made from ground-up _____.

7. _____ is a large, delicious, red fruit with a thick green rind.

9. The _____ of an egg is yellow and contains stored food for a bird or reptile before it hatches.

Down

1. _____ is a type of squash.

3. _____ is a liquid that we drink and use to wash. _____ Covers over two thirds of the surface of the earth, and much of our body is made of _____.

4. _____s are sweet vegetables that grow underground.

6. A _____ is a deep hole in the ground from which you get water.

7. A _____ is used to beat eggs or batter.

8. A _____ is a cooking pot used in Asia.

School

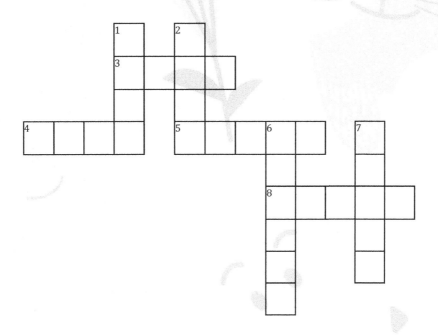

Across

3. A short form of a word that means a test given at school or a physical checkup.

4. Sheets of paper bound together between two covers. These pages can be blank or can have writing, printing, or pictures on them.

5. A stand for holding an artist's canvas, blackboard, or sign.

8. A book of maps, tables, or charts.

Down

1. A piece of furniture with drawers and a flat surface used for reading and writing.

2. A long narrow strip of plastic, cloth, or paper that has glue on one side. _____ is used to stick things together.

6. An object used to erase or rub out writing or marks.

7. A substance made from natural _____ that is formed into round sticks that can be used to write or draw with, especially on a blackboard or on pavement.

Science

Across

4. The study and application of scientific methods of soil management and field crop production; scientific agriculture.

6. The science that studies the growth and life processes of living things.

7. The scientific study of the relationships between living things and their environments.

8. The area of medicine that deals with the physiology and disorders of the urinary or genitourinary tracts.

Down

1. The science that studies the parts and structures of plants or animals.

2. The science of classification.

3. A system of studying, testing, and experimenting on things in nature. _____ is a search for general laws about how the world works.

5. The study of the physical structure of the earth and how it has changed over time. Geologists gain this knowledge by studying rocks. Some geologists study other planets.

Vacation

Across

4. A place with many rooms and beds where people pay money to sleep, eat meals, or buy other services.

5. A place where ships load and unload, and its nearby town or city.

7. A small house, usually built in a simple or rough way.

8. To go away from or depart.

Down

1. The land next to the ocean; seashore.

2. A cabin, hut, or other shelter meant to be used by people doing outdoor activities.

3. The land at the edge of a lake, ocean, or other body of water. A beach slopes gently toward the water and usually has sand or pebbles.

6. To rest while doing nothing or by spending time doing enjoyable things.

Season

Across

3. _____ is the second month of the year.

5. You can make a fire in a _____ to keep you warm.

6. _____ keep your ears warm.

Down

1. An _____ plant doesn't lose its leaves in the winter.

2. _____ is a game played at Hanukkah.

4. _____ is the twelfth month of the year.

5. _____ is the season between summer and winter. Another name for _____ is autumn.

7. Tree a fir is an evergreen tree; it doesn't lose its leaves in the winter.

Animals

Across

2. _____s are small mammals related to sloths and anteaters. They have a tough armor that protects them from enemies and other dangers.

3. _____ are large, hoofed mammals that people raise for their meat, milk, or hides. In some places _____ also pull carts or farm equipment.

4. _____ are among the most valuable of all domestic animals. Domestic animals are ones that have been tamed for use by humans. People eat _____ meat and drink _____ milk.

7. The _____ is a member of the horse family. The words _____ and ass are used to identify the same animal. However, the term _____ is used for domesticated, or ...

Down

1. The _____ is a mammal that people have valued for thousands of years. In the past people commonly used _____s to get from place to place and to pull heavy loads.

2. _____s are curious-looking animals. Their long heads and snouts look like tubes, and they have no teeth at all. _____s use their strong front legs and heavy claws.

5. _____s are stout, barrel-shaped mammals that are known for their big appetites. Some kinds of _____s are wild, while others are domestic (raised by humans).

6. _____s are horned mammals that can be either wild or tame. People keep _____s for their meat, milk, and wool. They are hardy animals that can live on coarse, thin grass.

Science

Across

3. The science of developing and caring for forests.
6. The medical science concerned with cancer, especially with tumors.
7. The scientific study of the microscopic structure of organic tissue.
8. The act or process of eating and using the nutrients in food for living and growing.

Down

1. The scientific study of viruses and of the diseases they cause.
2. The scientific study of human society, especially its origins, development, organization, and behavioral patterns.
4. The science that studies the form and function of basic elements and their compounds.
5. The scientific study and classification of rocks.

Vacation

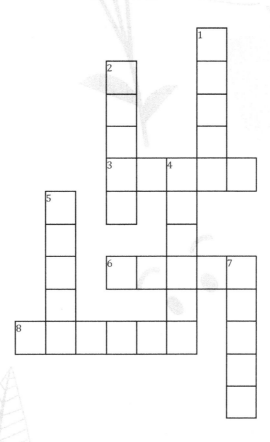

Across

3. A recording of pictures and sounds to be played on a television or computer.

6. A sheet that gives information in the form of a graph or table.

8. A trip on a plane from one place to another.

Down

1. To direct or lead along a way that is not familiar.

2. To travel in a car, truck or other private motor vehicle.

4. To leave; go away.

5. A path or course through a forest or other rural place.

7. The main stem of a tree.

Geography

Across

1. A _____ is a steep face of rock and soil.

3. A _____ is a narrow body of water that connects two larger bodies of water A _____ is also a part of a river or harbor that is deep enough to let ships sail through.

5. _____ is the study and the construction of maps.

Down

1. _____ is a meridian that passes through the center of a projection. The _____ is often a straight line that is an axis of symmetry of the projection.

2. A _____ is a large hole in the ground or in the side of a hill or mountain.

3. Projection a _____ is a type of map in which a cone is wrapped around a sphere (the globe), and the details of the globe are projected onto the conic surface. Then, the cone is unwrapped into a flat surface.

4. Rose a _____ is a design on a map that shows direction. It points which way is north, south, east, west, and some intermediate directions on the map.

Season

Across

3. _____ is a tree with pointy leaves and red berries.

4. Balls of ice that fall from clouds are called _____ or _____stones.

5. _____ is frozen water.

6. Some animals _____ during winter; they go into a very deep sleep-like state during freezing weather. They awaken only when the weather warms.

7. Some _____s keep your head warm. Some _____s are just for fun!

Down

1. A _____ is a large, slowly-moving river of ice.

2. _____ is a spicy cookie. _____ men and _____ women are cookies shaped like little people.

4. A _____ is a time to celebrate. Some _____s are new year's, mother's day, veteran's day, independence day, and thanksgiving day.

Animals

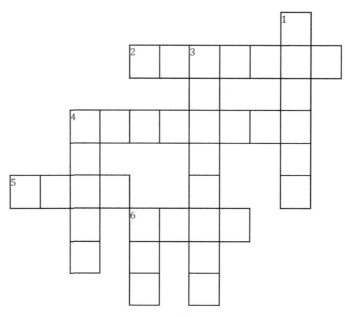

Across

2. _____s are small mammals that are related to mongooses. They are known for the way they stand upright to watch for enemies.

4. _____s are small mammals that live in the wild in Europe, Africa, and Asia. They are also kept as pets in some parts of the world.

5. _____ are mammals with thick, soft fur. People sometimes use the fur to make coats. There are two species, or types, of _____: the European _____ and the north American.

6. _____s are large, powerful mammals related to dogs and raccoons. The biggest _____s are the world's largest animals that live on land and eat meat. There are several ...

Down

1. _____s are mammals known for their powerful digging. They are related to weasels, skunks, otters, and mink. _____s live in many habitats.

3. _____s are the largest living land animals. There are three species, or kinds: the African Savanna _____, the African forest _____, and the Asian _____.

4. Badger the _____, or ratel, is a small mammal that is very strong and tough. It is a member of the weasel family, which includes skunks.

6. _____s are the only mammals that can truly fly. Sometimes people mistake _____s for birds. But _____s are more closely related to other mammals.

Vacation

Across

2. A meal eaten in the middle of the day, or any light meal during the day.
3. A round ball with a map of the earth on it, or anything shaped like a ball.
4. A thin material made from wood, rags, or grasses. _____ is used for writing, wrapping, and covering walls.
6. A tool for measuring the length of something. A _____ is marked off in inches, centimeters, or other units.

Down

1. To use the power of the mind.
2. To get to know or gain knowledge of through study or experience.
4. A person who is taught by a teacher.
5. Clever; intelligent.

Vacation

Across

3. A connected series of railroad cars.
7. A gap or break in activity, time, or space; interruption.
8. The land beside an ocean, sea, lake, or river.

Down

1. A small ship used for private trips or racing.
2. To go or come to see.
4. To go back or come back.
5. A short form of the word "airplane."
6. A long motor vehicle with many rows of seats used to carry large numbers of people. _____es usually travel along a regular route.

Geography

Across

4. A _____ is a unit of measurement; a _____ is also written °. There are 360 _____s in a circle. Each _____ is divided into 60 minutes, written as the symbol '. For example, 10 and a half _____s is written 10° 30'.

5. A _____ is a hill or a ridge made of sand. _____s are shaped by the wind, and change all the time.

6. _____ projection is a type of map in which a cylinder is wrapped around a sphere (the globe), and the details of the globe are projected onto the cylindrical surface.

8. A _____ is a line on a topographic map that represents locations that have the same altitude.

Down

1. The land mass on earth is divided into _____s.

2. A _____ is a very dry area.

3. A _____ is a low, watery land formed at the mouth of a river. It is formed from the silt, sand and small rocks that flow downstream in the river and are deposited in the _____. A _____ is often (but not always) shaped like a triangle (hence its name, _____, a Greek letter that is shaped like a triangle).

7. A _____ is small, horseshoe-shaped body of water along the coast; the water is surrounded by land formed of soft rock.

Season

Across

1. An _____ is a house made out of blocks of ice. Brr!
3. Skate when you wear _____s, you can glide across ice.
5. Sweaters and socks are made by _____.
6. _____ is a holiday that honors African American culture. _____ is celebrated from December 26 until January 1. The word "_____" means "first fruits" in Swahili

Down

1. An _____ is a huge chunk of ice that floats in the sea. Most of an _____ is hidden under the water.
2. _____ is the first month of the year.
3. _____s are hanging ice that are formed from dripping water.
4. A _____ is a short coat.

Animals

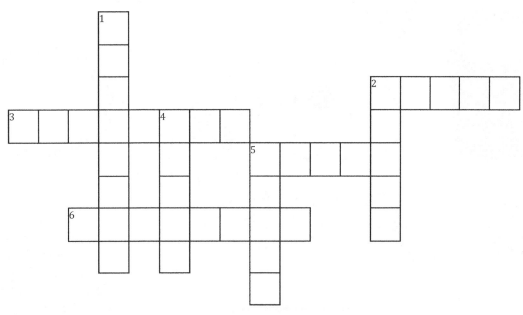

Across

2. _____s are black and white mammals known for their foul-smelling spray.

3. _____s are small, quick mammals that are known for killing cobras and other poisonous snakes.

5. Bear the _____ is a burly white bear that lives in the lands surrounding the north pole.

6. _____ rabbit is a small mammal that lives in South Africa. It is one of the most endangered animals in the world.

Down

1. _____s are shy mammals that are not seen very often. They are mostly active at night. _____s are also called scaly anteaters because they look like anteaters.

2. The animals called _____s look like mice. But unlike mice, _____s are not rodents. Instead _____s belong to a group of insect-eating mammals called insectivores.

4. _____s are mammals that live in and around water. Unlike most other animals, _____s are playful even as adults.

5. The name _____ is used for two mammals that live in Asia: the giant _____ and the lesser _____, or red _____.

School

Across

4. A long, thin tool used for writing or drawing. _____s are made of a narrow stick of graphite held within a case of wood.
6. A number or letter given on schoolwork to show quality or correctness.
7. A reply.
8. A place for teaching and learning.

Down

1. A piece of paper or cardboard folded at the center. A _____ can hold papers or letters.
2. A large, sturdy notebook cover that contains a device for holding loose papers.
3. A relaxing break from an activity, such as school classes or trials in court.
5. A period of instruction in a particular thing, or something that is intended to be learned or studied.

Geography

Across

2. A _____ is a long, narrow sea inlet that is bordered by steep cliffs.
4. _____ hemisphere consists of Africa, Asia, Australia, And Europe.
6. _____ is the scientific field that investigates how landforms are formed on the earth (and other planets).
8. An _____ is where a river meets the sea or ocean.

Down

1. A _____ is a map that notes the density, kind, size, and value of the trees in an area.
3. _____ map is a map that notes the structure and composition of geologic features, like the presence of minerals, rock types, earthquake faults, underground water, and landslide areas.
5. _____ is the study of the earth's surface.
7. The _____ is an imaginary circle around the earth, halfway between the north and south poles.

Winter

Across

2. _____s keep you warm at night.

4. _____s keep your hands warm.

6. A _____ is a short piece of a tree trunk.

7. An _____ will keep you warm when it is cold.

8. Year the beginning of a year is called the _____. People often celebrate on this day. A year consists of 12 months, 52 weeks, or 365 days.

Down

1. A _____ is a long, loose garment worn to bed.

3. _____ Bear are large meat-eaters live in the far north. They have clear-colored hair and black skin.

5. _____ Pole is the northernmost place on earth. There is no land at the _____, but there is a layer of ice on top of the arctic ocean around the pole.

School

Across

3. The act, art, or job of one who writes.
5. The language of this country or a manner of speaking that language. _____ is also standard in various other countries such as the united states.
6. A colored stick or pencil made of wax. A _____ is used for drawing and coloring.
7. An instrument for showing direction. A typical _____ has a moving magnetic needle that points north.
8. A person who goes to a school or college.

Down

1. Everything that has happened in the past to people or things, or a telling of these events.
2. One whose job is teaching; instructor.
4. A list of unusual or difficult words and their meanings connected with a particular subject or particular piece of writing. A _____ is often placed at the end of a book.

Vacation

Across

2. The top; peak; summit.

4. A day on which most people do not work so that they may honor and celebrate some person or event.

7. A building where collections of objects that are important to history, art, or science are kept and shown to the public.

8. To board a ship when beginning a trip.

Down

1. Fare for traveling by aircraft, especially by airplane.

3. A place where living animals, especially wild ones, are kept for people to look at. The word "_____" is short for "_____logical garden."

5. Freedom from work or other duties that take time and effort; free time.

6. To lead or go with on foot.

Geography

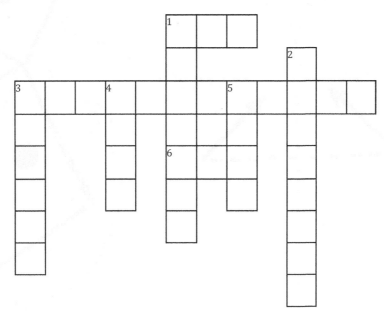

Across

1. _____ is short for global positioning system. _____ devices tell you your exact longitude and latitude (it gets the information from orbiting satellites).

3. Coordinate system a _____ is a system that uses latitude and longitude to describe points on the spherical surface of the globe.

6. ___ is an imaginary north-south line (at the 180th meridian), in the Pacific Ocean, at which the date changes. The east side of the _____ is a calendar day earlier than the west side. The actual _____ used is not a straight line, but zigzags around certain populated areas.

Down

1. A _____ is a slowly moving river of ice.

2. An _____ is a thick slab of floating ice that is next to land.

3. A _____ is a natural hot spring that occasionally sprays water and steam above the ground.

4. A _____ is a part of the ocean (or sea) that is partly surrounded by land (it is usually larger than a bay).

5. A _____ is a raised area or mound of land.

Season

Across

2. _____ is freezing rain.

3. There are four _____ in the year: winter, spring, summer, and fall (also called autumn).

4. When you _____, you glide over snow or water.

5. You can tie a bow in a _____ to decorate something.

Down

1. _____ live in the far north.

2. A _____ is a piece of cloth that people wear around their neck or on their head.

3. _____s are used to dig. A snow _____ is used to clear away snow.

4. _____ is flakes of frozen water that fall from clouds when it is very cold.

School

Across

4. A pack used to carry objects on one's back while hiking or walking.

5. A tool in a home or office that uses staples to attach papers together.

7. A person whose job or trade is printing.

8. The action or activity of examining and understanding written language.

Down

1. A pen, usually with a felt tip, that makes thick lines of ink and is used for writing and drawing.

2. A place where books, records, and other materials are kept and from which they may be borrowed.

3. A system of studying, testing, and experimenting on things in nature. _____ is a search for general laws about how the world works.

6. Any activity that takes great effort or planning.

Vacation

Across

3. Suitcases or trunks used to carry things during travel.

5. The act or process, or an instance, of leaving the ground or other surface, as in preparation for flight.

7. A place where people go to relax and have fun while on vacation.

8. To move about with no purpose, aim, or plan; roam.

Down

1. A long journey by air, land, sea, or outer space.

2. Something used to carry and move people or things.

4. An expedition for watching or hunting large animals.

6. A large area of level land where airplanes can land and take off.

Food

Across

1. A _____ is used for eating food like soup and cereal.

4. A _____ is a tool that has a wide, flat end.

5. A _____ is cheese, peanut butter, meat, or another filling between two slices of bread.

6. When something is _____d, thin pieces are cut from it.

7. _____ is an important crystalline mineral that we use to season our food.

Down

1. _____ grows in warm weather.

2. A _____ is a type of food that is usually made with lettuce and other vegetables.

3. _____ is a type of meat.

4. _____ is a type of salty, spicy meat product, usually made from beef and/or pork.

6. _____ is a slice of meat.

Food

Across

2. Breakfast, lunch, and dinner are _____s.

3. A _____ is candy on a stick.

5. A _____ is a sour, yellow fruit.

6. You can cut things with a _____.

7. Some people carry their lunch in a _____.

8. A _____ is a large spoon used to serve soup and gravy.

Down

1. _____ is a tube-shaped noodle.

3. _____ is a drink made from water, lemon juice, and sugar.

4. _____ is a meal eaten in the middle of the day.

8. A _____ is a sour, green citrus fruit.

Geography

Across

3. A _____ is a monument or some prominent object (like a mountain or lake) that is used to designate a place and determine one's location.

5. The _____ of a map (also called the legend) is a small table accompanying the map that explains the symbols that are used on the map.

6. An _____ is a piece of land that is surrounded by water.

7. An _____ is a narrow strip of land connecting two larger landmasses. An _____ has water on two sides.

8. The _____ of a map (also called the key) is a small table accompanying the map that explains the symbols that are used on the map.

Down

1. A _____ is a large body of water surrounded by land on all sides.

2. _____ is the angular distance north or south from the equator to a particular location. The equator has a _____ of zero degrees. The north pole has a _____ of 90 degrees north; the south pole has a _____ of 90 degrees south.

4. A _____ is a shallow body of water that is located alongside a coast and separated from the ocean by a strip of land or a sandbank.

Season

Across

2. _____s are made of snow - they are crystals. No two _____s look alike, but they all have six sides.

5. A _____ is very bad weather, like a blizzard or a thunder_____.

6. The _____ is air that blows outside.

Down

1. Snowmen are figures made from snow. They melt when the weather gets warm.

3. _____ is the state that the outdoors is in, like how windy it is, how hot or cold it is, or if it is raining or snowing.

4. Owl the _____ is a white owl that lives in the north American tundra (a cold, snowy environment).

5. _____ is the season after winter and before summer.

School

Across

2. A strip of leather, ribbon, or paper placed between pages to mark a place in a book.
3. An electronic device that is used to store and sort information and work with data at a high speed.
5. A row or rows of keys. Pianos, typewriters, and computers have _____s.
6. A way to communicate without using words.
7. That which separates, divides, or partitions.

Down

1. A chart of the days, weeks, and months of one or more years.
2. A set of shelves for holding books.
4. To learn completely so as to hold in the memory.

Vacation

Across

2. A way of acting that is usual or accepted for a person or a social group.

3. A major public road on which one can drive at high speeds, especially between cities.

5. Arrival upon the ground or other surface.

6. To travel across or through in order to discover or search for something.

7. The solid part of the earth's surface.

8. An outdoor area where tents or rough shelters are set up to live in or sleep in for a time.

Down

1. A light vehicle with two wheels, one behind the other, a small seat, and handlebars for steering. Pedals make the wheels move.

4. An escape, especially from the police.

Geography

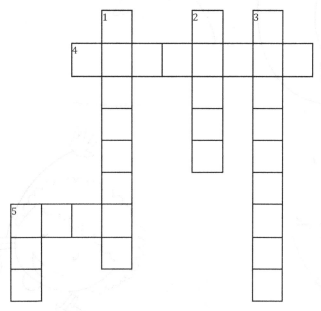

Across

4. _____ Projection is a type of rectangular map (a cylindrical projection) in which the true compass directions are kept intact (lines of latitude and longitude intersect at right angles), but areas are distorted,

5. A _____ is a land formation that has a flat area on the top and steep walls - _____s usually occur in dry areas.

Down

1. A _____ is a circular arc (a great circle) of longitude that meets at the north and south poles and connects all places of the same longitude. The prime _____ (0 degrees longitude) passes through Greenwich, England.

2. A _____ is a type of freshwater, brackish water or saltwater wetland that is found along rivers, pond, lakes and coasts. _____ plants grow up out of the water.

3. _____ is the angular distance east or west from the north-south line that passes through Greenwich, England, to a particular location. Greenwich, England has a _____ of zero degrees. The farther east or west of Greenwich you are, the greater your _____.

5. Scale the scale of a map is the ratio between the distance between two points found on the map as compared to the actual distance between these points in the real world.

Science

Across

1. The science of the earth's surface and all life on it. When studying _____, one learns about the different countries and people of the earth, its climate, its natural resources, and its oceans, rivers, and mountains.

6. A machine used in computing numbers.

7. A room in a school or college where classes are held.

8. A book of blank pages to keep notes in.

Down

2. To explore by trying different things.

3. A book, or a source of information found on a computer, that lists the words of a language in alphabetical order, along with information about their meaning, spelling, and pronunciation.

4. To ask for answers about something.

5. A tool for cutting paper, fabric, or the like, made up of two blades joined with a pivot so their edges may be opened and closed; _____.

Geography

Across

5. _____ Pole is the point on the northern hemisphere of the earth that is farthest north. It is 90° north of the equator.

6. A _____ is a map that shows weather conditions for a time period. _____s show storms, fronts, temperatures, rain, snow, sleet, fog, etc.

7. _____ Hemisphere is another name for the Americas (or the new world).

Down

1. A _____ is a very tall high, natural place on earth - higher than a hill. The tallest _____ on earth is mt. Everest.

2. _____ Hemisphere is the half of the earth that is north of the equator.

3. An _____ is a large body of salt water that surrounds a continent. _____s cover more the two-thirds of the earth's surface

4. An _____ is a place in the desert that has water and is fertile.

School

Across

4. _____ they have a smooth, shiny surface that is designed to be written on with special markers and easily erased.

6. A book that lists words with their synonyms or antonyms.

Down

1. To make thinner or finer, as a cutting edge or point.

2. The person who is head of a school.

3. A collection of unbound papers or other printed material, often constituting a sample of one's professional work, intended to be shown to others and transported from place to place in a specially designed case.

5. A measuring stick three feet long.

Geography

Across

2. _____ is a map that shows an areas natural physical features, like mountains, lakes, and rivers.

4. A _____ is a mountainous vent in the earth's crust.

5. A _____ (of latitude) is a line on a map that represents an imaginary east-west circle drawn on the earth in a plane _____ to the plane that contains the equator.

7. A _____ is a body of land that is surrounded by water on three sides.

Down

1. _____s are flat lands that have only small changes in elevation.

2. _____ is a map that represents only the horizontal positions of features (and not the vertical positions, like heights, which a topographic map shows).

3. _____ projection is a type of map in which the details of the globe are projected onto a plane (a flat surface) yielding a rectangular-shaped map.

6. A _____ is a large, flat area of land that is higher than the surrounding land.

Weather

Across

2. A tiny unit of plant or animal life, having a nucleus and surrounded by a very thin membrane.

3. Soft, mild, and soothing.

5. Not wet, damp, or moist.

Down

1. Without heat or warmth.

2. Not moving; still.

4. The mixture of gases that surrounds the earth. _____ is made up of oxygen, nitrogen, and other gases, and has no taste, odor, or color.

5. Little drops of water that collect at night on grass, plants, and other cool surfaces.

Weather

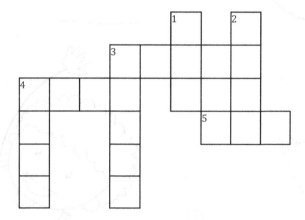

Across

3. An overflow of water onto land that is not normally under water.//
4. Without showing favor and without allowing an advantage for one side over another; just.//
5. The organ of the body that gives animals sight, and the area close around it.

Down

1. A thick mass, like a cloud, made up of tiny water drops floating in the air near the ground; mist.//
2. A small current of water, air, fog, or dust that spins against the main current.//
3. The most forward part or side of something.//
4. To drop downward from a higher place; descend.

Weather

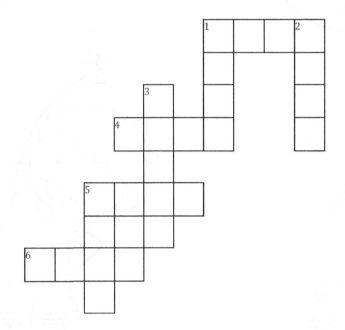

Across

1. Reaching up a great distance; tall.

4. A sudden rush or blast of wind.

5. Round pieces of frozen rain or a storm of this frozen rain.

6. A strong wind of about thirty to sixty miles per hour.

Down

1. A form of energy, or the state of being very warm; hotness; warmth.

2. Mist, smoke, or dust in the air, making it hard to see.

3. Having a high amount of water vapor; damp; moist.

5. A circle of light shining around the head of a god, an angel, or a saint in a picture.

Weather

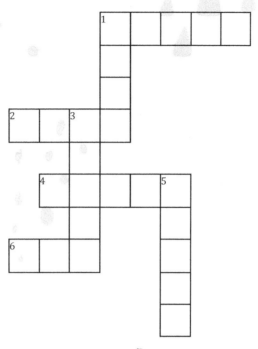

Across

1. Warm and damp so as to make breathing difficult.
2. A tying together of material such as rope, string, or yarn that is used to fasten.
4. Of or having to do with the north pole or south pole of the earth.
6. Water in a frozen, solid state.

Down

1. A mass or cloud of tiny water drops in the air.
3. A form of oxygen that occurs when oxygen is exposed to an electrical charge, like lightning. It is found naturally in earth's atmosphere.
5. The use of radio waves to track the location, distance, and speed of faraway objects. Waves are sent out and then picked up again when they bounce back after hitting some object.

Weather

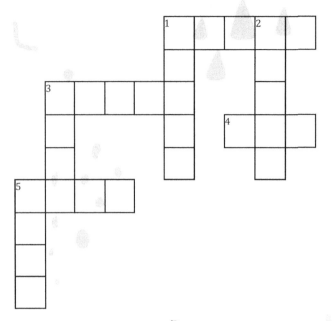

Across

1. Snow that is partly melted.
3. A long, narrow, raised section at the top of something; crest.
4. The air or space above the earth which appears to arch over it.
5. Soft, white flakes of ice that fall from the sky to the earth. _____ is formed when water in the upper air freezes into crystals.

Down

1. Freezing rain.
2. The visible black, gray, or white gases given off into the air by something that is burning.
3. Drops of water that form in the clouds and fall from the sky to the earth.
5. A mixture of smoke and fog that is caused by moist air and human pollution.

Weather

Across

3. Water vapor formed by boiling.

4. A strong forward motion; rush.

5. To go from being a frozen solid to being a liquid; melt.

Down

1. A mark or sign of a past event or thing.

2. A violent disturbance in the atmosphere that brings rain, snow, wind, thunder, or lightning.

4. To make larger by growth or pressure; expand.

Science

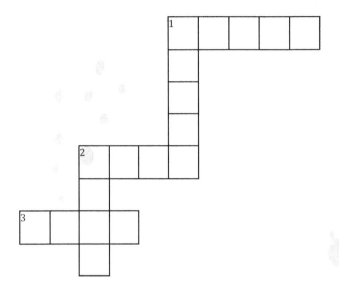

Across

1. To look closely or carefully.

2. A moving ridge or swell on the surface of a body of water.

3. An area that is divided from other areas because of a particular use or some other special quality.

Down

1. A piece of wood or metal shaped like a triangle with a thin edge. A _____ is driven or forced between objects to split, lift, or make them stronger.

2. Air as it moves naturally over the surface of the earth.

Geography

Across

3. A _____ is a chain of mountains and/or high elevations.

5. A _____ is a map that shows cultural features, like the political boundaries of countries, states, provinces, and cities.

6. A _____ is a wide, relatively flat area of land that has grasses and only a few trees.

7. A _____ is a representation of one thing onto another, such as a curved 3-dimensional surface (like the earth) onto a flat 2-dimensional map.

8. A _____ is a four-sided area bounded by two lines (parallels) of latitude and two lines of longitude (meridians) on a map.

Down

1. The _____ refers to either the arctic circle (in the northern hemisphere) or Antarctic circle (in the southern hemisphere).

2. The _____ (0 degrees longitude) is the meridian that passes through Greenwich, England.

4. A _____ is a small body of water surrounded by land. A _____ is smaller than a lake.

Geography

Across

2. _____ Projection is a widely-used type of map in which the earth is shown within an ellipse with a flat top and bottom.

3. A _____ is a large body of salty water that is often connected to an ocean. A _____ may be partly or completely surrounded by land.

4. A _____ is a large, flowing body of water that usually empties into a sea or ocean.

6. A _____ is a topographic map that uses different colors or shades to indicate elevations.

Down

1. _____ map shows major and minor highways, plus cities and towns. This type of map is used by road travelers, and often shows other information useful for travelers, including parks and campgrounds.

2. A _____ is a man-made lake that stores water for future use.

4. A _____ is an undersea growth of coral near the surface of the water.

5. The _____ of a map is the ratio between the distance between two points found on the map as compared to the actual distance between these points in the real world.

Geography

Across

2. _____ Level is height of a sea or ocean.
3. A _____ is a narrow body of water that connects two larger bodies of water.
5. Hemisphere the _____ is the half of the earth that is south of the equator.
6. A _____ is an area of land that is often wet; the soil in _____s are often low in oxygen. _____ plants are adapted to life in wet soil. There are many types of _____s, including: swamp, slough, fen, bog, marsh, moor, muskeg, peatland, bottomland, Delmarva, mire, wet meadow, riparian, etc.

Down

1. A _____ is a low place between mountains.
2. The _____ is the point on the southern hemisphere of the earth that is farthest south. It is 90° south of the equator.
3. A _____ is a wide inlet of the sea or ocean that is parallel to the coastline; it often separates a coastline from a nearby island.
4. A _____ is the beginning of a river.

Geography

Across

4. A _____ is a stream or river that flows into a larger river.

5. The _____ is the warm, equatorial region between the tropic of cancer and the tropic of Capricorn.

6. A _____ is a type of freshwater wetland that has spongy, muddy land and a lot of water. Many trees and shrubs grow in _____s.

Down

1. A _____ is a map that represents elevations on it.

2. _____ of Capricorn is an imaginary line of latitude at 23°30' s.

3. When a river falls off steeply, there is a _____.

4. A _____ is a cold, treeless area; it is the coldest biome.

People

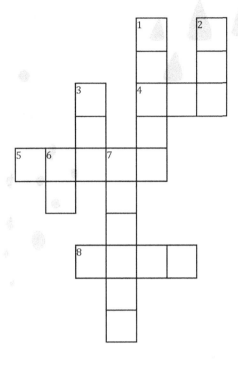

Across

4. Boys grow up to be men.

5. Being a _____ is a person.

8. A _____ is a hereditary ruler of a country.

Down

1. Girls grow up to be women.

2. _____ are your relatives.

3. _____ is another word for mother.

6. _____ is a word that means yourself and others.

7. An _____ creates works of art.

Shapes

Across

2. A _____ is a doughnut-shaped object.

6. A _____ is a four-sided figure. The square, rectangle, rhombus, trapezoid, kite, and parallelogram are _____s.

7. A _____ is a shape that has a point at one end and a circular opening at the other end.

Down

1. A _____ has four, equally long sides which are at right angles to each other.

3. An _____ is an eight-sided figure. Stop signs are _____s.

4. A _____ is a many-sided figure with straight edges.

5. A _____ is round.

8. A ball-shaped object is an _____.

House

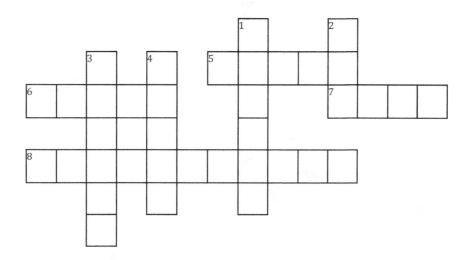

Across

5. A _____ is a type of barrier.

6. A _____ is a piece of furniture that people sit on.

7. You can go in and out through a _____.

8. A _____ has a mechanical bird that sings every hour.

Down

1. A _____ is a pot in which you boil water. Key

2. People sleep in _____s.

3. You can turn water flow on or off at a _____.

4. You can sweep the floor with a _____.

Spring

Across

1. April showers bring may ____
4. Grass grows and turns the color ____
6. Hold this to stay dry when it rains
8. Fly a ____ on a windy day

Down

2. Temperature that is not too cold and not too hot
3. A yellow flower that faces the sun
5. Children go to the ____ and play
7. Plant a ____ and wait for a flower to grow

Science

Across

5. When a liquid is changing to a gas
7. When a solid is changing to liquid form
8. How shiny or dull an object is

Down

1. 2 or more atoms joined together
2. _____ change when matter changes and creates a new matter
3. The amount of space an object takes up
4. Matter that does not have a definite shape or volume. The atoms are very loose.
6. The smallest amount of matter in an object

Adjectives

Across

2. When you are very mad.

3. It is above average size.

6. They are not the same.

8. It is blue during the day.

Down

1. When we are afraid.

4. It is not clean.

5. When you are not sick.

7. Empty is the opposite of it.

Measurement

Across

4. Determining the physical quantity of something such as length, time, temperature, or volume in terms of a unit of _____ such as feet, seconds, or degrees.

6. The measurement of the surface of an _____ is defined in square units. The _____ is the number of squares that fit inside the region. The formula for determining the _____ of a rectangle is length x width.

7. When guessing a measurement close to the exact measurement, this is called an _____.

8. A _____ is a tool used to measure distance. It can also help to draw straight lines.

Down

1. A device for measuring temperature.

2. The _____ is the path that surrounds an area. The distance of the path is the measurement of the _____.

3. The length between two points as drawn by a straight line.

5. A _____ of measurement is a standard by which measurements can be compared. Different types of measurements use different _____s.

Geography

Across

3. The height above sea level or above the earth's surface.
6. The process of a liquid converting to the gaseous state. _____ is a type of vaporization of a liquid, which occurs only on the surface of a liquid.
7. _____ is obtained by hydrolysis of starch. It is a tasteless, odorless gummy substance that is often used as a thickening agent, in adhesives and in dietary supplements.
8. Complex proteins produced by cells that facilitates or speeds up certain bio-chemical reactions in the body.

Down

1. _____ is a type of aquatic plant often called the waterweeds. _____ is native to north America and is also widely used as aquarium vegetation.
2. A mixture of gases (especially oxygen) required for breathing; the stuff that the atmosphere consists of.
4. A substance that promotes drying.
5. An instrument for measuring atmospheric pressure, used especially in weather forecasting, but is also used to measure altitude.

Mathematics

Across

4. A number is divisible if it can be divided without leaving a remainder.

5. -the remainder is the amount left over after a division operation.

6. The numbers that are added together in addition problems.

7. When dividing, the dividend is the number that is getting divided or broken up.

Down

1. In division, the divisor is the number by which the dividend is divided.

2. This is the number that is subtracted in a subtraction operation.

3. The quotient is the answer to a division operation. The quotient does not include the remainder, if there is one.

4. A mathematical operation where a number is split into equal groups.

Body Parts

Across

2. It is a clean pad that is used to cover and protect cuts and other injuries.

4. It is a special, high-energy picture of your bones or teeth.

7. It is the part of the face that is above the eyebrows and below the hair.

8. We have ten toes on our _____.

Down

1. It is the outer covering of our body.

3. It is a science that studies the body.

5. It pumps blood throughout your body.

6. These are the sides of the face between the mouth area and the ear.

Astronomy

Across

5. It is the gas that surrounds a planet.
7. It happens when the moon blocks out light from the sun or the earth's shadow goes across the moon.
8. They are tiny planets that mostly orbit between mars and Jupiter.

Down

1. _____ moon is smaller than a half moon.
2. It orbits the earth.
3. It is a cloud of gas and dust in space.
4. It is a meteoroid that has entered the earth's atmosphere, usually making a fiery trail as it falls. It is sometimes called a shooting star. Most burn up before hitting the earth.
6. It is a distant energy source in space which gives off large amounts of radiation.

Sports

Across

2. _____s are used to hit a golf ball.

4. A baseball _____ is a glove used to catch balls.

6. In _____, you shoot an arrow (using a bow), aiming at a target.

8. A _____ is an award that you can wear.

Down

1. The _____ games began over 2700 years ago in ancient Greece.

3. _____ is played with an oddly-shaped ball in the USA.

5. _____ is one of the martial arts.

7. When you take a _____, you travel on something else, like a bicycle, a horse, or other means of transportation.

Letters

Across

1. You can write a _____ to communicate with a person.
4. A _____ is where you leave letters to be mailed.
7. A _____ is a card you can mail without an envelope. People who collect post cards are called deltiologists.
8. We write and paint on _____. It is made from plant fibers, usually trees.

Down

2. An _____ holds a letter.
3. You can send a _____ to a friend.
5. A _____ is a wrapped box that contains something.
6. An _____ tells the post office where to bring a letter or package.

Fire Fighting

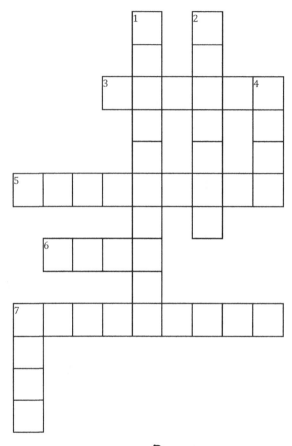

Across

3. You can climb up a _____ to reach tall things.
5. An _____ takes sick people to the hospital.
6. A _____ is a symbol of a group of people, like a country or an organization.
7. Fire fighters travel on a _____ to put out fires.

Down

1. A _____ helps you find your way in the dark.
2. Fire fighters hook a hose up to a fire _____ to get water.
4. A _____ is useful for tying things together.
7. _____ is very hot.

Devices

Across

4. It presses the wrinkles out of clothes.

5. It helps you find your way in the dark.

6. They designs and creates new, useful things.

7. A clothes _____ is used to hold up an item of clothing in a closet.

Down

1. It is a device that lets you pour things from one container to another.

2. It is a spinning wheel set in a movable frame. When the wheel spins, it is very hard to move the gyroscope - it essentially stays in its original orientation.

3. It is used to play some computer games.

5. It keeps things icy.

Science

Across

2. _____ meter is a unit for measuring the volume of a solid.

5. A unit for measuring volume.

6. _____ point is the temperature at which matter changes from a liquid to a solid.

7. The amount of material that an object has in it.

Down

1. Two or more substances that are mixed together but can be easily separated.

3. _____ point is the temperature at which matter changes from a liquid to a gas.

4. A change in matter that produces a different kind of matter.

Ocean

Across

3. _____ is a plant that lives in the sea.
4. _____ live in the water and breathe with gills.
5. When you _____, you move around in the water.
6. _____ is brown seaweed that grows in cold water.
8. The _____ is the main body or frame of a ship.

Down

1. There are _____s of water in the ocean.
2. An _____ is a playful aquatic mammal.
3. _____ are small animals that live in the water.
5. Some animals grow a _____ for protection.
7. _____s are birds that live near oceans and lakes.

Food

Across

1. _____ is a sweet substance made by bees.
3. _____s are used for eating solid food.
4. _____ is the part of some plants that contains the seeds. Apples, strawberries, oranges, and bananas are _____.
5. A _____ keeps things icy.
6. _____ is a spicy cookie. _____ men and _____ women are cookies shaped like little people.
7. We drink out of _____es.

Down

1. A _____ is a cooked patty of ground beef, usually served in a bun.
2. _____s are a type of citrus fruit that sometime squirt you when you eat them.
3. You can cook food in a _____.
4. The _____ (or food chain) is all of the interactions between predators and prey in which plants and animals obtain food.

Shapes

Across

2. A _____ is a ball-shaped object.
4. A _____ is a four-sided figure with two parallel sides.
6. A _____ is a very small dot.
7. An _____ is an egg-shaped figure.
9. A _____ is a seven-sided figure.
10. A _____ has three sides.

Down

1. _____s are patterns within patterns within patterns.
3. An _____ is a twenty-sided regular geometric solid.
5. _____ things are curved. A circle is _____.
8. A _____ is a curve that winds in on itself. Snail shells have a _____ pattern.

House

Across

3. _____ are cloth hung on and around a window.

5. A _____ is a door in a fence.

6. This fireplace is made out of _____s.

8. You can make a fire in a _____ to keep you warm.

9. Some people live in _____s.

Down

1. A _____ is a machine that makes a breeze.

2. A _____ is a piece of furniture in which you can store things.

3. _____ is well-made pottery that was first made in _____.

4. An _____ is a chair with arms.

7. An _____ is a house made out of blocks of ice. Brr!

Weather

Across

4. Water falling from the sky
8. A person whose job it is to plant crops
9. A caterpillar turns into a _____
10. Open the ___ and let fresh air into the house

Down

1. _____ rain gathers in one spot on the ground and makes a _____
2. Colorful arc in the sky after the rain
3. A place to plant flowers or plants
5. Birds make a _____ to lay eggs
6. Spring starts during this month
7. Ice and snow _____

Matter

Across

1. How much matter is in an object

4. When a liquid is changing to a solid form

5. _____ change when matter changes how it looks but not what it is made of

8. The combining of different matter without changing what the matters are

9. Measures temperature

10. Matter that has a definite shape and volume. The atoms are packed tightly together.

Down

2. The combination of equal amounts of matter

3. The size, shape, luster, color, texture of an object

6. A kind of matter that does not have a shape but has volume. The atoms are loose.

7. Anything that has mass and takes up space

Adjectives

Across

3. It has many colors.
5. When things look the same.
8. When you are scared.
10. People usually smile

Down

1. It is the color of wood.
2. It is not open.
4. When you are not asleep.
6. It occurs before it was expected to happen.
7. You can make this color by mixing blue and yellow color
9. The opposite of it is thin.

Mathematics

Across

2. _____ is a three-dimensional measurement of a cube with all three sides the same size. It is represented by a small 3 next to the number like x^3.

5. A unit of measure used for angles.

7. The measurement of the distance of a side of an object. Usually this is the shorter side while the length is the longer side.

9. The measurement of an object that expresses its hotness or coldness. The units of measurement are degrees Fahrenheit or degrees Celsius.

10. _____ a number or measurement is when you write the number in a shorter or simpler form that is an approximation of the exact number or measurement.

Down

1. A measurement of distance. It is usually the longer of two distances of an object, the other being the width.

3. _____ area is the total of three-dimensional object is the added areas of all the objects surfaces (for a cube this would be 6 sides).

4. The measurement of the vertical distance.

6. In measurement, the _____s are represented by length, width, and height.

8. The quantity of space that an object takes up. It is measured in cubic units.

Ocean

Across

3. A sperm whale secretion. Sperm whales produce it to protect their stomachs from the beaks of the cuttlefish they swallow, and formerly valued greatly in the manufacturing process of perfumes.
7. Tiny particles with a negative charge that are capable of creating an electrical current.
8. An electronic device that changes, usually increases, the strength or amplitude of a signal passing through it.
9. _____ is a physical property of a substance, caused by the intermolecular attraction between like-molecules within a body or substance that acts to unite them.
10. A _____ is a material intended to assist cleaning. The term is sometimes used to differentiate between soap and other surface-active chemical cleaning agents widely used in industry and laundering.

Down

1. A chemical that can bind two incompatible items, such as oil and water.
2. The _____ of a human is a muscle located on the upper arm. The _____ has several functions, the most important being to rotate the forearm and to flex the elbow.
4. To make larger or more powerful; increase.
5. Any polymer having the elastic properties of rubber.
6. A minute rudimentary plant contained within a seed.

Body Parts

Across

1. We have five these on each hand.
3. It is the widest finger on a person's hand. It is next to the pointing finger. All apes (like gorillas and chimps) have these.
6. It is a pouch-like organ that is part of the digestive system. It helps digest food by churning it in an acid bath.
7. People have five _____, the _____ of sight, hearing, touch, smell, and taste.
9. We use these to chew food.

Down

2. These are a part of the digestive system. These helps digest food, absorb it into the body, and excrete waste.
4. These let you open and close your mouth and take bites.
5. It is the part of the face below the mouth.
7. The _____ (also called the backbone) is a series of connected bones in the back that surround and protect the spinal cord.
8. It is the joint in the middle of your arm.

Astronomy

Across

3. It is the seventh planet from the sun. Uranus looks bluish and is covered with clouds. It has an unusual, tipped axis, which gives it extreme seasons.
7. They goes up into space to explore.
9. It is a group of stars that we see in the sky. They are not necessarily located together in space but looks as though they are from earth.
10. It is the third planet from the sun. It's where we live!

Down

1. It is a dwarf planet that is usually farther from the sun than any of the planets
2. These are beautiful lights in the near-polar sky.
4. They are people who study astronomy and learn about objects in the universe, like stars and planets.
5. It is a reddish planet and the fourth planet from the sun. It is the planet that comes closest to the earth.
6. It is an enormous group of stars.
8. It is a small, icy object that orbit the sun. It's tail always points away from the sun.

Sports

Across

2. When you _____, you go up and down.
4. A _____ is used to hit a ball or shuttlecock in sports like tennis and badminton.
6. A _____ is the target used when playing darts.
8. A _____ is a small ball used in golf - the ball sits on a tee in the grass.
9. When you wear _____s, you can roll along the ground.

Down

1. _____ is a sport in which you get points for throwing a ball into a basket.
3. The _____ include aikido, judo, karate, taekwondo, and other sports.
5. A _____ is a small, pointed object that is thrown at a target in a game.
7. When you _____, you are not still.

Fire Fighting

Across

2. _____ is a liquid that can put out some types of fires.
3. A _____ is a tool that turns nuts or bolts, like those on a fire hydrant.
6. An _____ is useful for chopping wood.
7. The _____ is a white dog that has dark spots.
8. Water flows through a _____.
9. _____ are a type of shoe. _____ cover the feet and part of the lower legs.

Down

1. A _____ is a fire.
4. A _____ is an ax with a short handle.
5. You can get hurt in a _____ous situation.

Ocean

Across

1. A _____ is a northern marine mammal with ivory tusks.
2. The _____ is a large, shelled animal from warm seas.
4. A _____ is a small, slow animal with its own shell.
5. _____s are gentle, slow-swimming, aquatic mammals.
6. _____s are gentle, slow-swimming, aquatic mammals.
8. A _____ has a hard shell and eyes on stalks on its head.

Down

1. _____s are ocean animals with a hard, spiral shell.
3. _____s are birds that cannot fly but swim very well.
4. A _____ is a primitive animal that lives in the water.
7. _____s are birds that are sometimes called "sea swallows."

Food

Across

3. _____ is pressed from fruit or vegetables.
4. A _____ is a type of cooked meat in the shape of a sausage; it is usually served in a long bun.
5. The _____ is a tangy fruit that grows in warm areas.
7. _____ is cold, creamy, and sweet treat.
8. A _____ is a pot in which you boil water.
9. _____ is a spread made from fruit.

Down

1. When you're _____, you want to eat some food.
2. People prepare and store food in a _____.
6. _____ is a cold drink.
7. _____ is frozen water.

People

Across

3. _____s are young children.

5. A _____ is a hereditary ruler of a country.

6. An _____ shoots an arrow with a bow.

8. A _____ is a man who has a child.

9. A _____ can help you when you're sick or hurt.

Down

1. A _____ takes care of you when you are sick or hurt.

2. An _____ is a girl or woman who has inherited or will inherit a lot of money.

3. A _____ is someone who helps you learn.

4. An _____ is a baby.

7. A _____ is a woman.

Shapes

Across

4. A _____ is the shape of the moon around the time of the new moon.
5. A _____ is a shape that has many points.
7. A _____ is a twelve-sided regular geometric solid composed of pentagons.
8. A _____ is half a circle.
9. Polyhedra are solids made from polygons.
10. A _____ is a five-sided figure

Down

1. A _____ is a four-sided figure in which the two pairs of adjacent sides have the same length.
2. An _____ is an eight-sided regular geometric solid.
3. A _____ is a wavy line or surface.
6. A _____ is a four-sided figure whose opposite sides are parallel.

Devices

Across

2. A _____ keeps things icy.
4. Tables, chairs, sofas, and beds are _____.
7. A _____ is a device that opens cans.
8. _____s hold garbage.
10. A _____ is a structure in which you can build a fire.

Down

1. A _____ is a large, free-standing pendulum clock.
3. People put pictures and photos in _____s to protect them and make them look nice.
5. We use _____s to lock and unlock doors.
6. Things are stored in _____s.
9. _____ is where you live.

Science

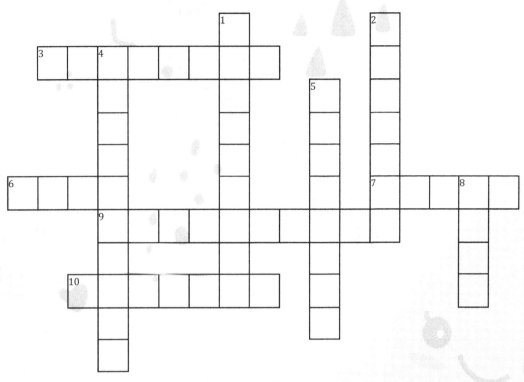

Across

3. Very small living organisms made of only one cell which are present everywhere (the air, the soil, on the skin).

6. The opposite of an acid. A _____ has a ph-level of more than 7.0 up to 14.0 (a ph of 7 is neutral)

7. _____ is the tendency of a solid material such as soil, to slowly move or deform permanently under the influence of certain forces.

9. The opposite of 'evaporate'. The transition from a gaseous state into a liquid state.

10. A unit of measurement of the refractive power of a lens, which is equal to the reciprocal of the focal length measured in meters.

Down

1. A '_____', also called an 'ecospheres', is a mostly closed ecosystem of a specific size that contains a mix of plants and animals that is completely self-sufficient.

2. A state of equilibrium

4. The transfer of heat through a fluid (liquid or gas) caused by molecular motion. In the atmosphere, _____ usually refers to the vertical movement of air masses.

5. The ability of water to support weight allowing an object to float.

8. The repetition of a sound resulting from reflection of the sound waves.

Body Parts

Across

2. These are hard scales that grow at the ends of your fingers.
3. These are bean-shaped organs that take waste from the blood and produce urine.
6. It is the set of bones in a body.
8. It is the bony structure of head that encloses the brain and supports the jaws.
9. We use it to eat and talk.

Down

1. It is an animal that walks on two legs.
2. It is between your head and your shoulders.
4. These are long hairs on the edges of the eyelids.
5. It is the joint between your foot and leg.
7. We have five toes on each of these.

Astronomy

Across

4. It is the eighth planet from the sun. This frozen planet has 8 moons.

6. _____ system has eight planets, one dwarf planet, many asteroids, comets, and other objects orbit around our sun.

7. Astronauts wear this when they walk in space.

9. It is place where people observe the skies, using a device like a telescope.

Down

1. It is a meteor that has fallen to earth. These are made of stone, iron, or stony-iron.

2. It is the second planet from the sun and the hottest planet in our solar system.

3. Everything is made up of tiny _____

5. It put on star shows that teach astronomy.

6. Each of the these we see in the night sky is another sun, but much farther away than our sun.

8. It is a band of 12 constellations (groups of stars) in the sky, including Capricorn, Aquarius, Sagittarius, Scorpio, Libra, Virgo, Leo, Cancer, Gemini, Taurus, Aries, and Pisces.

Ocean

Across

1. _____s swim in the oceans. They have ten arms and an ink sac.
4. _____s are animals with two shells. They burrow under the sand.
5. The _____ is a large fish with an almost circular, flattened body.
6. The _____ is an arctic whale; the male has a huge tooth.
9. _____s are large marine mammals. _____s breathe air using lungs.

Down

1. _____ are fish that live in the sea and spawn in fresh water.
2. _____ are organs that fish and amphibians use to breathe underwater.
3. The _____ is fish-eating bird with a huge, pouched bill.
7. An _____ is a heavy metal device that holds a ship in place.
8. _____s are warm, clear, shallow ocean habitats that are rich in life.

Food

Across

3. Breakfast, lunch, and dinner are _____s.
4. A _____ is a large spoon used to serve soup and gravy.
6. A _____ is candy on a stick.
8. You can cut things with a _____.
9. Some people carry their lunch in a _____.

Down

1. _____ is a tube-shaped noodle.
2. A _____ is a sour, green citrus fruit.
5. A _____ is a sour, yellow fruit.
6. _____ is a drink made from water, lemon juice, and sugar.
7. _____ is a meal eaten in the middle of the day.

People

Across

4. _____ were Japanese warriors.
5. A _____ bakes food in the oven, like breads, cakes, and cookies.
8. _____s are boys or men who have the same parents.
9. _____ diver swims under the water and carry their own air in a tank on their back.

Down

1. A _____ is a group of related people.
2. A _____ is a young woman.
3. An _____ is an unelected ruler of a country.
6. A _____ is a human being.
7. A _____ is a young person.
10. A _____ is a very young person.

Shapes

Across

5. A _____ is a four-sided figure whose sides are at right angles to each other.

6. A _____ is a pyramid formed by four triangles.

7. A _____ is a figure with a long round body.

9. A _____ is a parallelogram with equal-length sides.

Down

1. The _____s in Egypt are huge buildings that have a square base and triangular sides.

2. The _____ is a shape that often symbolizes love.

3. A _____ is a six-sided figure. Bee hives have _____al cells.

4. A _____ is a folded geometric figure that can be flexed to expose its many sides.

7. A _____ is a solid geometric figure with six square faces.

8. An _____ is a flattened circle.

Devices

Across

3. You take a bath in a _____.

5. _____ are cloth hung on and around a window.

6. Books are stored in _____s.

8. _____s are used to hang wet laundry on a clothes line to dry.

9. A few people can sit on a _____.

Down

1. A _____ is a small, simple shelter.

2. Plants grow in a _____.

4. A _____ is a small piece of furniture.

7. A _____ is a floor covering made of woven yarn or thick fabric.

8. A _____ is a big, soft piece of furniture that many people can sit on.

Conclusion

Thank you again for buying this book! I hope you enjoyed with my book. Finally, if you like this book, please take the time to share your thoughts and post a review on Amazon. It'd be greatly appreciated! Thank you!

Next Steps
– Write me an honest review about the book –
I truly value your opinion and thoughts and I will incorporate them into my next book, which is already underway.

Get more free bonus here

www.funspace.club

Follow us : facebook.com/funspaceclub

Send email to get answer & solution here : funspaceclub18@gmail.com

Find us on Amazon

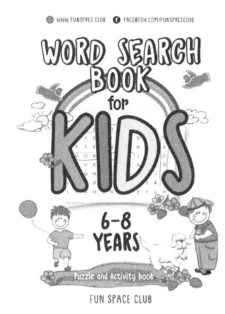
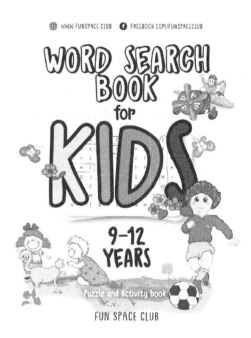
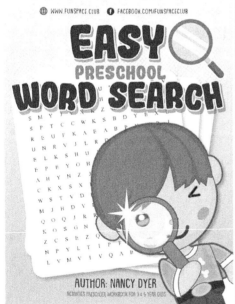
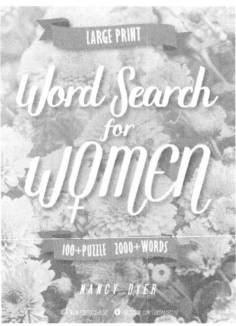

Find us on Amazon

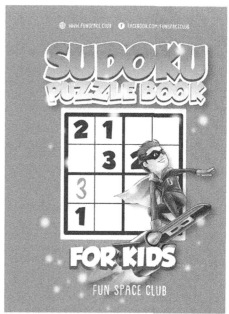

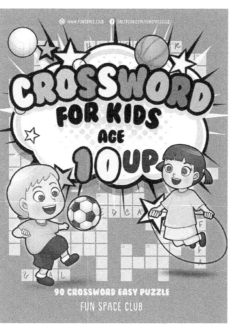

Made in the USA
Middletown, DE
15 September 2020